Pegan Diet Recipes

Insanely Powerful Recipes To Boost Your Energy And Put
An End To Cravings

(Find Out All You Need To Know About The Pegan Diet)

Alan Lloyd

TABLE OF CONTENTS

Introduction

If you're thinking about going Pegan, you're thinking smart my friend because going Pegan means going clean, going fresh, and going oh so deliciously good. Peganism is the happy marriage of the Paleo and Vegan lifestyles.

The Paleo lifestyle is a throwback to eating the way our ancestors did thousands of years ago. Clearly, our Paleolithic ancestors were not noshing on Twinkies and microwave pizzas since processed foods are a relatively new invention, thanks to modern-day machinery.

Prior to processed pseudo-food, meals required foraging the land and foods were eaten fire-cooked or raw. The typical diet would have been composed of fruits, vegetables, nuts, and animal protein.

The other half of the Pegan lifestyle is composed of elements of the Vegan diet. Vegans do not consume animal proteins, nor do they consume animal products like yogurt and eggs. Instead, their diet relies heavily on clean whole foods like veggies, fruits, nuts, and grains.

In this book we have brought together the best of both worlds to introduce you to the Pegan lifestyle. The Pegan cookbook is filled with delicious recipes for breakfast, lunch, dinner, appetizers, and snacks that take into consideration all of the elements of the Pegan diet.

These dishes will keep you healthy, satiated, and glowing. Have pink grapefruit with Coconut Lime Dressing for a delicious antioxidant boost in the morning, or perhaps some Coconut Pancakes with Peaches and Walnuts for a decadent brunch on Sunday.

The lunch offerings are divine, if I do say so myself. Enjoy Pistachio Jewel Salad for a taste of the unbeknownst kind, or some Hearty Cabbage and Fennel Soup.

When the dinner bell gongs, whip out the grill and enjoy a Portabella Mushroom Salad with an appetizer of Almond Honey Cauli-Skewers.

And you won't have to skip dessert, since the offerings are healthy but also mucho delicious—like our designer Strawberry Cashew Cake.

Overnight Oats

INGREDIENTS

- 1/2 plum
- 4 basil leaves
- 2 tablespoons chia
- ¾ cup rolled oats
- 2 cup vanilla cashewmilk
- 1/2 cup peach
- 2 tsp pumpkin seeds
- 2 tsp hemp seeds

DIRECTIONS

1. In a bowl mix cashewmilk, oats, chia and oats, divide into 1-5 servings
2. Refrigerate overnight

4

Remove and serve

Avocado Brownie

INGREDIENTS

- 2 tablespoon vanilla extract
- ¾ cup cocoa powder
- 1 tsp salt
- 1 cup gluten-free flour
- 1/2 cup dark chocolate chips
- 2 ripe avocado
- 4 tablespoons melted butter
- 2 fresh egg
- 1/2 cup brown sugar
- 1/2 maple syrup

DIRECTIONS

1. Preheat the oven to 450F
2. In a bowl mash the avocado, brown sugar, maple syrup, vanilla, sugar, water, butter, add cocoa powder
3. In a bowl mix salt and flour and stir in avocado mixture, spread bake in the pan and bake for 50 minutes
4. Remove and cool before serving

Breakfast Mix

INGREDIENTS

- 1/2 cup cocoa cereal
- 1/2 cup rice cakes
- 2 cup corn cereal
- 2 cup rice cereal

DIRECTIONS

In a bowl combine all ingredients together

Serve with milk

Sausage Breakfast Sandwich

INGREDIENTS

- 2 turkey sausage patty
- 2 tablespoon cheddar cheese
- 1/2 cup fresh egg substitute
- 2 muffin

DIRECTIONS

1. In a skillet pour fresh egg and cook on low heat
2. Place turkey sausage patty in a pan and cook for 5-10 minutes per side

On a toasted muffin place the cooked egg, top with a sausage patty and cheddar cheese

Serve when ready

Breakfast Granola

INGREDIENTS

- 2 lb. rolled oats
- 2 tablespoons sesame seeds
- 1/2 lb. almonds
- 1/2 lb. berries
- 2 tsp vanilla extract
- 2 tablespoon honey

DIRECTIONS

. Preheat the oven to 450F

2. Spread the granola onto a baking sheet
3. Bake for 25-30 minutes, remove and mix everything
4. Bake for another 25-30 minutes or until slightly brown
5. When ready remove from the oven and serve

Raspberry Crumble

INGREDIENTS

2 fresh eggs

2 cup raspberries

2 cup apple juice

2 cup oats

2 tablespoon butter

2 tablespoon brown sugar

2 tablespoon cinnamon

1/2 tsp cloves

DIRECTIONS

1. Preheat oven to 490 F
2. In a bowl combine raspberries, apple slices and apple juice
3. In another bowl combine sugar, spices, oats, butter and mix well
4. Cover apple slices with crumble topping
5. Bake for 50-55 minutes
6. When ready remove and serve

Quinoa Crepes With Applesauce

INGREDIENTS

- 2 tsp cinnamon
- 2 cup water
- 2 tablespoons canola oil
- 2 cups organic apple sauce
- 2 cup quinoa flour
- 1 cup tapioca flour
- 2 tsp baking soda

DIRECTIONS

1. In a bowl combine quinoa flour, baking soda, cinnamon, tapioca flour, water, oil and whisk well

2. Preheat a skillet over medium heat and pour 1/2 cup batter into skillet

3. Cook each crepe on low heat for 1-5 minutes per side

4. When ready remove and serve with apple sauce

Cheese Omelette

INGREDIENTS

- 2 tablespoon olive oil
- 1/2 cup cheese
- 1/2 tsp basil
- 2 cup low-fat cheese
- 2 fresh eggs
- 1/2 tsp salt
- 1/2 tsp black pepper

DIRECTIONS

In a bowl combine all ingredients together and mix well

In a skillet heat olive oil and pour the fresh egg mixture

3. Cook for 1-5 minutes per side
4. When ready remove omelette from the skillet and serve

Cucumber Omelette

INGREDIENTS

- 2 tablespoon olive oil
- 1/2 cup cheese
- 1/2 tsp basil
- 2 cup cucumber
- 2 fresh eggs
- 1/2 tsp salt
- 1/2 tsp black pepper

DIRECTIONS

In a bowl combine all ingredients together and mix well

In a skillet heat olive oil and pour the fresh egg mixture

Cook for 1-5 minutes per side

When ready remove omelette from the skillet and serve

Banana Pancakes

INGREDIENTS

- 1/2 tsp baking powder
- 2 cup mashed banana
- 2 fresh eggs
- 2 cup milk
- 2 cup whole wheat flour
- 1/2 tsp baking soda

DIRECTIONS

5. In a bowl combine all ingredients together and mix well
6. In a skillet heat olive oil
7. Pour 1/2 of the batter and cook each pancake for 1-5 minutes per side
8. When ready remove from heat and serve

18

Buckwheat Pancakes

INGREDIENTS

- 2 tsp baking powder
- 2 cup almond milk
- 2 tablespoon canola oil
- 2 bananas
- 2 cup buckwheat flour
- 2 tablespoon brown sugar
- 1/2 tsp salt

DIRECTIONS

1. In a bowl combine dry ingredients
2. Add wet ingredients and mix well
3. In a skillet pour 1/2 cup batter and cook for 1-5 minutes per side

When ready remove and serve with
syrup

Morning Cookies

INGREDIENTS

- 4 bananas
- 1/2 cup peanut butter
- 1/2 cup cocoa powder
- handful of salt

DIRECTIONS

1. Preheat oven to 450F
2. In a bowl mix all ingredients
3. Form small cookies and place them onto
   a greased cookie sheet

4. Sprinkle with salt and bake for 25-30 minutes

5. Remove and serve

Blueberry Bites

INGREDIENTS

- 1 cup honey
- 1 cup almond butter
- 2 tsp vanilla
- 2 cups oats
- 1 tsp cinnamon
- 2 cup blueberries

DIRECTIONS

. Mix all of the ingredients together, except for the blueberries.

. Fold in the blueberries and refrigerate for 45 minutes.

. Form balls from the mixture and serve.

Ginger Lemonade

INGREDIENTS

- 1/2 cup honey
- 4 lemons juice
- Ice
- 4 strips of lemon peel
- 2 tbs ginger root
- 2 sprigs rosemary

DIRECTIONS

1. Mix the honey, ginger, lemon peel and 2 sprigs rosemary in a pot with 2 cups water.

Bring to a boil, then simmer for 25 minutes.

Remove from heat and allow to cool for 30 minutes.

Strain into a pitcher.

Discard the ginger and rosemary.

Add 6 cups of cold water and lemon juice to the pitcher.

Stir to combine and serve with ice.

Lime Grilled Corn

INGREDIENTS

- Pepper
- 2 tbs lime juice
- 1/2 tsp chili powder
- 4 corns
- 2 tbs mayonnaise
- Salt

DIRECTIONS

1. Preheat the grill.
2. Cook the shucked corn onto the grill for 10 minutes.
3. Turn every few minutes until all sides are charred.
4. Mix the mayonnaise, chili powder, and lime juice in a bowl.

Season with salt and pepper and add lime juice and chili powder.

Serve coated with the mayonnaise mixture.

Apple Crumble

INGREDIENTS

- 2 cup flour
- 1 cup walnuts
- 2 cups quinoa
- 1/2 cup ground almonds
- 4 apples
- 2 tsp cinnamon

DIRECTIONS

1. Preheat the oven to 480F.
2. Oil a baking dish.
3. Place the apples into prepared dishes.
4. Mix the remaining ingredients in a bowl.
5. Crumble over the apples.
6. Bake for 45 minutes.
7. Serve immediately.

Gingersnaps

INGREDIENTS

- 1/2 cup molasses
- 4 tbs Swerve
- 1/2 tsp salt
- 2 tbs butter
- 2 fresh egg white
- 2 1/2 tsp vanilla
- 2 tsp stevia
- 2 tsp baking powder
- 2 ¾ cups flour
- 2 ¾ ground ginger
- 1/2 tsp ground cinnamon
- 2 /8 tsp nutmeg
- 2 /8 tsp cloves
- 4 tsp cornstarch

- 1/2 cup milk

DIRECTIONS

1. Preheat the oven to 450 F.
2. Mix the cornstarch, nutmeg, flour, cloves, ginger, cinnamon, baking powder, and salt in a bowl.
3. In another bowl, whisk the butter, egg, vanilla, and stevia.
4. Stir in the molasses and milk.
5. Incorporate the flour mixture.
6. Divide into 50 portions and roll into balls.
7. Roll in the Swerve until coated.
8. Place on a lined baking sheet.
9. Sprinkle with Swerve and bake for 25 minutes.
10. Allow to cool, then serve.

Rice Krispies

Serves: *30*
Prep Time: *25*   Minutes

31

Cook Time: *60* Minutes
Total Time: *8 0* Minutes

INGREDIENTS

4 cups rice cereal

2 tbs dark chocolate

2/4 cup honey

1 cup peanut butter

Salt

2 tsp vanilla

DIRECTIONS

1. Combine all of the ingredients except for the dark chocolate in a bowl.
2. Spread the mixture on a lined baking pan.
3. Drizzle the melted chocolate on top.

Refrigerate for 2 hour.

Cut into bars and serve.

Breakfast Cookies

Serves: 8-8
Prep Time: 6   Minutes
Cook Time: 30   Minutes
Total Time: 25   Minutes

INGREDIENTS

2 cup rolled oats

1/2 cup applesauce

1 tsp vanilla extract

4 tablespoons chocolate chips

2 tablespoons dried fruits

2 tsp cinnamon

DIRECTIONS

1. Preheat the oven to 450F
2. In a bowl combine all ingredients together and mix well
3. Scoop cookies using an ice cream scoop
4. Place cookies onto a prepared baking sheet
5. Place in the oven for 25-30 minutes or until the cookies are done
6. When ready remove from the oven and serve

SMOOTHIES

Tangerine Smoothie

Serves: 2
Prep Time: 6   Minutes
Cook Time: 6   Minutes
Total Time: 25 Minutes

INGREDIENTS

2 tangerines

2 cup pineapple

2 banana

2 cup ice

DIRECTIONS

1. In a blender place all ingredients and blend until smooth
2. Pour smoothie in a glass and serve

MOCKTAIL

Serves:	*2*
Prep Time:	*25* Minutes
Cook Time:	*0* Minutes
Total Time:	*25* Minutes

INGREDIENTS

Ice

6 ounces soda water

4 lime slices

8 mint leaves

2 tbs honey

DIRECTIONS

Add mint leaves and lime to a glass and muddle with a spoon.

Add honey, ice and soda.

Stir to combine.

Serve garnished with lime and mint.

Peanut Butter Smoothie

Serves: 2
Prep Time: 6   Minutes
Cook Time: 6   Minutes
Total Time: 25   Minutes

INGREDIENTS

2 cup strawberries

2 banana

2 tablespoons peanut butter

DIRECTIONS

1. In a blender place all ingredients and blend until smooth

2. Pour smoothie in a glass and serve

Carrot Smoothie

Serves: 2
Prep Time: 6   Minutes
Cook Time: 6   Minutes
Total Time: 25   Minutes

INGREDIENTS

2 carrot

2 mango

2 tablespoons coconut flakes

DIRECTIONS

1. In a blender place all ingredients and blend until smooth
2. Pour smoothie in a glass and serve

Ginger Smoothie

Serves: 2
Prep Time: 6   Minutes
Cook Time: 6   Minutes

Total Time: *25* Minutes

INGREDIENTS

2 cups pineapple

2 tablespoons lime juice

2 -pice ginger

DIRECTIONS

. In a blender place all ingredients and blend until smooth

. Pour smoothie in a glass and serve

Kale Smoothie

Serves: 2
Prep Time: 6 Minutes
Cook Time: 6 Minutes
Total Time: 25 Minutes

INGREDIENTS

2 cup kale

2 cup cherries

2 cup blueberries

DIRECTIONS

1. In a blender place all ingredients and blend until smooth

Pour smoothie in a glass and serve

Mango Smoothie

Serves: 2
Prep Time: 6   Minutes
Cook Time: 6   Minutes
Total Time: 25 Minutes

INGREDIENTS

2 cup mango

2 cup cherries

2 cup Greek yogurt

DIRECTIONS

1. In a blender place all ingredients and blend until smooth
2. Pour smoothie in a glass and serve

MUFFINS

Simple Muffins

Serves:	8-8	
Prep Time:	25	Minutes
Cook Time:	25	Minutes
Total Time:	45	Minutes

INGREDIENTS

2 fresh eggs

2 tablespoon olive oil

2 cup milk

2 cups whole wheat flour

2 tsp baking soda

1/2 tsp baking soda

2 cup pumpkin puree

2 tsp cinnamon

1/2 cup molasses

DIRECTIONS

1. In a bowl combine all wet ingredients

2. In another bowl combine all dry ingredients

3. Combine wet and dry ingredients together

4. Pour mixture into 8-8 prepared muffin cups, fill 2/4 of the cups

5. Bake for 2 8-25 minutes at 490 F

6. When ready remove from the oven and serve

Cornbread Muffins

Serves: *4*
Prep Time: *25*   Minutes
Cook Time: *25*   Minutes
Total Time: *45*   Minutes

INGREDIENTS

2 cup whole-wheat flour

2 can of Whole Kernel Corn 30 oz.

1 cup milk

2 fresh egg

1 cup butter

2 tablespoon honey

2 tablespoon baking powder

2 tsp salt

DIRECTIONS

1. Preheat oven to 490 F

Blend corn until smooth

In a bowl mix baking powder, salt and flour

In another bowl mix eggs, butter, corn, milk and honey

Pour over the flour mixture and mix well

Pour mixture into a cupcake pan and bake for 30 -25 minutes

Morning Muffins

Serves: *8-8*
Prep Time: *25*   Minutes
Cook Time: *26*   Minutes
Total Time: *50*   Minutes

INGREDIENTS

2 cup oats

1/2 cup unsweetened applesauce

2 fresh egg whites

2 cup oat milk

2 cup whole wheat flour

1/2 cup brown sugar

1/2 tsp baking soda

1/2 tsp salt

2 tsp cinnamon

1 cup blueberries

DIRECTIONS

1. Preheat oven to 490 F
2. In a bowl combine all ingredients together and mix well
3. Fill 8-8 paper muffin cups with batter and fold in blueberries
4. Bake for 20-26 minutes, serve when ready

Fiber Muffins

Serves: *8-8*
Prep Time: *6*   Minutes
Cook Time: *30*   Minutes
Total Time: *25*   Minutes

INGREDIENTS

2 cup wheat bran

2 cup nonfat milk

1/2 cup unsweetened applesauce

2 fresh egg

1/2 cup brown sugar

1/2 cup all-purpose flour

1/2 cup whole wheat flour

2 tsp baking powder

2 tsp baking soda

1/2 tsp salt

2 cup blueberries

DIRECTIONS

1. Preheat oven to 450 F
2. In a bowl combine wheat bran and milk and set aside
3. In another bowl combine egg, brown sugar, apple sauce and stir in bran mixture, mix well
4. In another bowl combine baking soda, baking powder, wheat flour, all-purpose flour and mix well
5. Stir flour mixture into bran and fresh egg mixture and mix well
6. Fold in blueberries and fill muffin cups with batter
7. Bake for 25-30 minutes
8. When ready remove and serve

Strawberry Muffins

Serves: 8-8
Prep Time: 25   Minutes
Cook Time: 25   Minutes
Total Time: 45   Minutes

INGREDIENTS

2 fresh eggs

2 tablespoon olive oil

2 cup milk

2 cups whole wheat flour

2 tsp baking soda

54

1/2 tsp baking soda

2 tsp cinnamon

2 cup strawberries

DIRECTIONS

In a bowl combine all wet ingredients

In another bowl combine all dry
ingredients

Combine wet and dry ingredients
together

Fold in strawberries and mix well

Pour mixture into 8-8 prepared muffin
cups, fill 2/4 of the cups

Bake for 2 8-25 minutes at 490 F,
remove when ready

Oven-Baked Haddock with Mango Salsa

Servings: 4

Ingredients:

- 4 (6-ounce) boneless haddock fillets
- Olive oil, as needed
- Salt and pepper to taste
- 2 large ripe mango, pitted and diced
- 1 cup diced seedless cucumber
- 2 tablespoons minced red onion
- 2 tablespoons fresh chopped cilantro
- 2 tablespoon fresh lime juice

Instructions:

1. Preheat the oven to 4 6 0°F.
2. Brush the fillets with olive oil then season with salt and pepper to taste.
3. Place the fillets on a roasting pan and bake for 25 to 30 minutes until the flesh flakes easily with a fork.

Combine the remaining ingredients in a bowl, tossing to combine.
Serve the fillets hot with the mango salsa.

Grilled Portobello Mushroom Burgers

Servings: 4

Ingredients:

- 4 large Portobello mushroom caps, stems removed
- 2 1 tablespoons balsamic vinegar
- 4 tablespoon olive oil
- 2 teaspoon raw honey
- Salt and pepper to taste

Instructions:

1. Whisk together all of the ingredients except for the mushrooms in a small bowl.
2. Place the mushrooms in a shallow dish and cover with the marinade.
3. Let the mushrooms soak for 45 minutes.
4. Preheat the grill to medium heat and brush the grates with olive oil.

Place the mushrooms on the grill and cook for 6 to 6 minutes per side, basting with marinade often, until tender.

Serve the mushrooms on toasted buns with your favorite burger toppings.

Spaghetti Squash with Sautéed Veggies and Fish

Servings: 4

Ingredients:

- 2 large spaghetti squash
- 2 tablespoon olive oil
- 2 medium yellow onion, chopped
- 2 teaspoon minced garlic
- 4 (4 to 6-ounce) boneless white fish fillets
- 2 cups Brussels sprouts, trimmed and quartered

Instructions:

1. Preheat the oven to 400°F.
2. Cut the spaghetti squash in half and scoop out the seeds.
3. Place the squash halves cut-side down in a baking dish and pour in just enough water to cover the bottom.

Roast the squash for 45 to 410 minutes until fork-tender.

Remove the squash from oven and then shred the squash into a bowl with a fork.

Heat the oil in a medium skillet over medium heat.

Add the onion and garlic and cook for 4 to 4 minutes until translucent.

Push the onion and garlic to the sides of the skillet and add the fish.

Cook the fish for 4 to 10 minutes on each side until the flesh flakes easily with a fork.

0. Stir in the Brussels sprouts and cook for 4 to 4 minutes until lightly browned.

1. Toss in the spaghetti squash and season with salt and pepper to taste. Serve hot.

Quinoa and Beef-Stuffed Roasted Peppers

Servings: 6

Ingredients:

- 6 assorted bell peppers
- 2 tablespoon olive oil
- 1 lbs. grass-fed ground beef
- 2 medium yellow onion, chopped
- 4 cups diced mushrooms
- 2 cups fresh chopped spinach
- 2 medium green pepper, cored and diced
- Salt and pepper to taste
- 2 cups cooked quinoa

Instructions:

1. Preheat the oven to 4 6 0°F and grease a rectangular glass baking dish.

Slice the tops off the peppers and remove the seeds and membrane.

Arrange the peppers upright in the baking dish.

Heat the oil in a large skillet over medium-high heat.

Add the beef and onion and cook for 6 to 8 minutes until the beef is browned.

Drain most of the fat from the skillet.

Stir in the mushrooms, spinach and peppers then season with salt and pepper to taste.

Add the quinoa and stir well then spoon the mixture into the peppers.

Cover the dish with foil and bake for 45 minutes.

). Turn the dish and bake for another 25 to 45 minutes until the peppers are tender.

Cornmeal Waffels

Serves: *2*
Prep Time: *25*   Minutes
Cook Time: *25*   Minutes
Total Time: *25*   Minutes
INGREDIENTS

2 cup corn flour

2 fresh egg

2 cup milk

2 tablespoon butter

2 tablespoons honey

1 cup rice flour

2 tsp baking powder

1 tsp salt

DIRECTIONS

Let sit for 8-25 minutes

Place in the waffle iron and cook

Remove and serve

Cheese Cake

Serves: *4*
Prep Time: *25*   Minutes
Cook Time: *45*   Minutes
Total Time: *40*   Minutes

INGREDIENTS

1 lb. gingernut biscuits

1 lb. blueberries

2 tsp vanilla extract

2 tsp acid

1/2 lb. butter

1/2 lb. caster sugar

2 tablespoons arrowroot

1/2 lb. full-fat Philadelphia

2 fresh eggs

DIRECTIONS

1. Preheat oven to 4 6 0 F
2. In a bowl mix butter and biscuits and press into the base of the tin
3. Bake for 25-30 minutes
4. In a saucepan cook blueberry with sugar and milk for 25-30 minutes
5. Take off heat add citric acid and vanilla
6. Bake for 40 minutes remove and let it chill

Basic Waffles

Serves: 2
Prep Time: *25*   Minutes
Cook Time: *25*   Minutes
Total Time: *25*   Minutes

INGREDIENTS

2 fresh eggs

2 tablespoon sugar

2 tablespoon baking powder

2 cup flour

2 /8 cup milk

1 tsp vanilla essence

DIRECTIONS

In a food processor add all the ingredients and blend until smooth

Heat the waffle iron pour in the batter

Cook until golden

Serve with maple syrup

Caramel Popcorn

Serves: *4*

Prep Time:	*25*	Minutes
Cook Time:	*25*	Minutes
Total Time:	*45*	Minutes

INGREDIENTS

2 tablespoon olive oil

4 tablespoons popcorn kernels

CARAMEL SAUCE

2 tablespoon butter

2 tablespoon brown sugar

2 tablespoon golden syrup

DIRECTIONS

1. In a saucepan pour olive oil and popcorn kernels over medium heat and cover

2. Shake the saucepan to distribute evenly

In another saucepan melt the caramel sauce ingredients

Remove from heat and pour over your popcorn

Onion Pancakes

Serves: *4*
Prep Time: *25* Minutes
Cook Time: *25* Minutes
Total Time: *25* Minutes

INGREDIENTS

1 tsp salt

2 cup plain flour

2 tsp olive oil

2 onion

1 cup hot water

2 tablespoon cold water

DIRECTIONS

1. In a bowl mix all ingredients
2. Pour mixture into a pan and cook for 1-5 minutes per side
3. Remove and serve

Toasted Muesli

Serves: 4

Prep Time: *25*   Minutes
Cook Time: *60*   Minutes
Total Time: *80*   Minutes

INGREDIENTS

2 cups oats

2 cup oat mix

1 cup sunflower seeds

1 cup sunflower oil

DIRECTIONS

In a bowl mix all ingredients

Bake for 60 minutes at 28 6 F

Garnish with blueberries and serve

Gingerbread Biscuits

Serves: *4*
Prep Time: *25* Minutes
Cook Time: *45* Minutes
Total Time: *40* Minutes

INGREDIENTS

2 oz. butter

2 cup self raising flour

1 tsp salt

4 tablespoons ginger

1 cup milk

2 fresh egg beaten

2 tablespoon vanilla extract

1 cup golden syrup

1 cup maple syrup

1 cup honey

DIRECTIONS

Preheat oven to 450 F

In a pan melt honey, butter, syrup and set aside

White syrup mixture is cooling, grate the ginger and add to the syrup mixture

Add flour, salt, milk, fresh egg and vanilla extract

Form small cookies and bake for 25-30 minutes at 450 F

Remove and serve

Vanilla Chia Pudding

INGREDIENTS

- 1 tsp cinnamon
- 1 cup chia seeds
- 2 tablespoon vanilla extract
- 2 cups hemp milk

76

- 2 packets stevia

DIRECTIONS

. In a bowl whisk all ingredients together
. Let it chill overnight and serve

Apple Pancakes

INGREDIENTS

- 2 cup apples
- 2 fresh eggs
- 2 cup milk
- 2 cup whole wheat flour
- 1/2 tsp baking soda
- 1/2 tsp baking powder

DIRECTIONS

1. In a bowl combine all ingredients together and mix well
2. In a skillet heat olive oil
3. Pour 1/2 of the batter and cook each pancake for 1-5 minutes per side

78

When ready remove from heat and serve

Cinnamon Almond Apple Crisp

Ingredients:

4 tablespoons raw honey
4 large eggs, beaten well
4 tablespoon ground cinnamon
2 teaspoon ground nutmeg
1 teaspoon salt

6 ripe apples (Granny Smith), peeled and sliced thin
2 cup coconut flour
2 cup shredded coconut, unsweetened
1 cup melted coconut oil

Instructions:

1. Preheat your oven to 4 6 0°F.
2. Spread the sliced apples in a pie plate as evenly as possible.
3. Place the remaining ingredients in a food processor and pulse until well combined.
4. Spread the mixture over the apples then bake for 45 to 50 minutes until the apples are tender and the topping is browned.
5. Cool for 25 minutes then serve the apple crisp drizzled with coconut cream.

Creamy Zucchini Soup

Ingredients

¾ cup red lentils
2 cup coconut milk
4 cups water
2 teaspoon salt
2 teaspoon black pepper
Olive oil
6 zucchinis, peeled and chopped
2 medium onion, chopped
4 cloves garlic, minced

Directions

Soak red lentils in warm water for 25 minutes.
Heat 4 tablespoons olive oil in skillet over medium.

3. Add garlic and onion, sauté for one minute.
4. Rinse lentils and place in slow cooker, along with onion, garlic, zucchini, water, and salt.
5. Cook on high for 4 hours.
6. Stir in coconut milk and cook for another 25 minutes.
7. Using an immersion blender, mix until smooth.

Citrus Avocado Salad

Ingredients

1 cup almonds, chopped
4 cups lettuce, chopped
1 teaspoon salt
1 teaspoon black pepper
8 ounces pasture-raised chicken breast

2 oranges
2 avocado, pitted and sliced

Directions

Peel and segment oranges, combine with avocado, walnut, salt, and black pepper.
Plate lettuce, top with the orange-avocado mixture.
Shred chicken breast with fork and divide evenly among salad plates.

The Pegan Wrap

Ingredients

4 cups almond flour
¾ cup water
Rapeseed oil
1 teaspoon salt
1 teaspoon baking powder

Filling

1 cup walnuts, chopped
2 teaspoon oregano
2 teaspoon salt
2 teaspoon black pepper
2 cups white kidney beans
4 red, yellow, and green bell peppers,
seeded and sliced
2 red onion, sliced
Olive oil

Directions

Combine flour, salt, and baking powder in a bowl, slowly add water, mixing to form a ball.

Knead dough on flat surface, and divide into 6 balls.

Use a rolling pin to roll out the tortillas.

Heat non-stick pan on medium, and cook tortillas for 5 minutes per side.

For the filling heat 4 tablespoons olive oil in skillet, add onions, sauté for a minute, add bell peppers and sauté for 10 minutes.

Sprinkle with salt, black pepper, and oregano.

Fill wraps and serve.

Creamy Cauliflower And Chicken Breast

Ingredients

2 cup coconut milk
2 teaspoon paprika
2 teaspoon salt
Coconut oil
8 ounces pasture-raised chicken breast, cubed
2 large head cauliflower
2 large carrots, sliced into discs

Directions

1. Preheat oven to 450°F and lightly coat a casserole dish with a little coconut oil.
2. Slice cauliflower into florets and mix with carrot discs, salt, and paprika.
3. Place cauliflower in casserole dish and pour coconut milk on top.

. Cover with aluminum foil, and bake for 50 minutes.
. For the chicken, heat 4 tablespoons coconut oil in skillet, add chicken breast cubes and sauté for 10 minutes, or until no longer pink inside.
. Enjoy chicken breast pieces along with creamy cauliflower.

Stuffed Peppers

Ingredients

2 teaspoon oregano
1 teaspoon cinnamon
2 teaspoon salt
2 teaspoon black pepper
Olive oil
8 ounces grass-fed lean ground beef

4 green bell peppers

2 cup cauliflower, grated

1/2 cup sundried tomato

2 medium onion, minced

4 cloves garlic, minced

2 cups tomato puree

Directions

1. Heat 2 tablespoons olive oil in skillet, add onion and garlic and sauté for one minute.
2. Place half of the mixture into a slow cooker, along with tomato puree, and mix.
3. Add beef to skillet, brown, and drain.
4. Mix beef and onion with grated cauliflower and sundried tomatoes, salt, black pepper, cinnamon, and oregano.
5. Slice the tops off the peppers, remove seeds, and stuff peppers with cauliflower mixture.

Place peppers in the slow cooker and cook on low for 8 hours.

Pesto Noodles

Ingredients

6 zucchinis
Salt
Black pepper
Extra virgin olive oil
2 cups basil, fresh
4 tablespoon pine nuts
2 cloves garlic

Directions

Using a mandolin slicer, make long noodles of zucchini.
Place in a mixing bowl, and stir in 4 tablespoons extra virgin olive oil and 1 teaspoon salt, set aside.

3. Combine basil, pine nuts, 1 teaspoon salt, 1 teaspoon black pepper, and1/2 cup extra virgin olive oil in a blender, and mix until smooth.
4. Serve pesto over zucchini noodles.

Chick Peas With Veggie And Bean Sprout Sauté

Ingredients

2 stalk celery, diced
2 medium onion, sliced
4 cloves garlic, minced
4 cups bean sprouts
2 teaspoon black pepper

1 cup coconut aminos
2 cups chick peas, cooked
2 cup broccoli florets
2 cup cauliflower florets
2 carrot, sliced
Olive oil

Directions

Heat 4 tablespoons olive oil in skillet, add onion, garlic, and sauté for one minute.

Add veggies, except bean sprouts, and sauté for 10 minutes or until tender.

Add bean sprouts and sauté for another 4 minutes.

 Mix in coconut aminos.

Divide sprout mixture among plates, top with chick peas, and serve.

Lavender Zucchini Wrap

Ingredients

1 teaspoon black pepper
Coconut oil, melted
4 Pegan Wraps
4 zucchinis
1/2 cup lavender flowers
1 teaspoon salt

Directions:

1. Slice zucchinis in half.
2. Combine lavender flowers, salt, black pepper, and 4 tablespoon coconut oil.
3. Place zucchini in marinade and let sit for one hour.
4. Heat grill to medium-high, and cook zucchinis for 10 minutes per side.

Sweet 'N' Salty Chia Pudding

Ingredients

2 heaped tablespoons cashew butter,
1/2 teaspoon salt
6 dates, pitted, chopped
6 tablespoons chia seeds
¾ cup unsweetened almond milk
1/2 cup pure maple syrup

Method

Place all the ingredients in a bowl. Whisk
well. Refrigerate for a few hours
Serve chilled.

Banana Cream Pie Blizzards

Ingredients

2 0-8 medjool dates, pitted, if dry, soak in hot water for 25 minutes, drain
1/2 cup banana powder (ground banana chips)
1/2 cup coconut oil, melted
2 bananas, sliced
2 cups raw cashews, soaked for 6 hours, drained
2 cups unsweetened almond or coconut milk
2 teaspoons pure vanilla extract
A few vegan cookies, crushed

Method

Blend together all the ingredients except ripe banana to a smooth and creamy puree. Transfer the contents to an ice cream bowl and freeze until done.

. Serve ice cream with sliced bananas.

No-Bake Caramel Chocolate Slice

Ingredients

1/2 cup raw cacao powder
2 tablespoons maple syrup
1/2 cup coconut milk
2 teaspoons vanilla extract
2 cups cashews, soaked in hot water for 25 minutes

26 Medjool dates, pitted, soaked in hot water for 25 minutes

1/2 cup coconut oil, melted

2 teaspoons raw cacao powder

2 teaspoons vanilla extract or essence

Pinch of salt

¾ cup almond flakes, toasted

For the chocolate layer

1 cup coconut oil

Method

1. Blend together all the fudge ingredients except half the almond flakes to a sticky fudge mixture in a large mixing bowl.
2. Transfer the fudge into a square tin lined with parchment paper.
3. Smooth with a spatula. Refrigerate for an hour to chill.
4. Meanwhile, place all the chocolate layer ingredients except the raw cocoa powder in a double boiler.

When it is well blended, add cocoa powder and whisk well until smooth. Remove from heat.

Pour the chocolate sauce over the fudge. Smooth the top with a spatula.

Sprinkle the remaining almond flakes. Refrigerate for 5-10 hours before serving.

Quick Coconut & Chia Seed Pudding

Ingredients

2 teaspoons vanilla extract

1 teaspoon Himalayan pink salt or to taste

2 cup fresh raspberries

1 cup unsweetened coconut, shredded

1 cup chia seeds

2 1 cups full fat coconut milk

2 cup coconut water

Method

1. Mix together all the ingredients except raspberries in a bowl.
2. Refrigerate for 3-4 hours.
3. Serve with raspberries.

Three-Layer, Nut-Free Dream Cups:

Ingredients

For the bottom layer:
6 tablespoons melted coconut butter

For the middle layer:

4 tablespoons pure maple syrup
1/2 cup virgin coconut oil, softened
2 teaspoon vanilla extract
A pinch of fine sea salt
1 cup sunflower seed butter

For the top layer:

- 1 cup virgin coconut oil, melted
- 1 cup unsweetened cocoa powder
- 1/2 cup maple syrup
- A pinch of fine sea salt
- 6 tablespoons unsweetened large flake coconut

Method

1. Line a 10 muffin pan with paper liners.
2. Add about a teaspoon of melted coconut butter to each of the mold. Freeze the molds.
3. To make the middle layer: Mix together all the ingredients.
4. Add a tablespoon of the filling to each of the frozen molds.
5. Freeze again.
6. To make the top layer: Whisk together all the ingredients except large flake coconut.

Add a tablespoon of the filling to each of the frozen molds. Finally, add a teaspoon of large flake coconut. Freeze again until set and serve.

Coconut Pancakes With Peaches And Walnuts

Ingredients

1/2 cup coconut flour

2 teaspoon baking powder

2 cup almond milk

1 teaspoon vanilla extract

1/2 teaspoon salt

Coconut oil

2 peaches, pitted

1/2 cup organic honey, divided

1/2 cup walnuts, chopped

2 fresh eggs

Directions

For topping, slice peaches, mix with 2 tablespoons of honey and the walnuts, and set aside.

For pancakes, whisk eggs, combine with almond milk, 2 tablespoons honey, salt, vanilla extract, and 2 tablespoon of coconut oil in a bowl.

In a second bowl, sift coconut flour and baking powder.

Slowly add the wet mixture into the dry mixture while mixing.

Lightly coat a skillet with coconut oil and place over medium heat.

Pour approximately 1/2 cup of batter into skillet and cook approximately 5 minutes per side.

 You will flip the pancakes over when little bubbles form.

Top with fruit and enjoy!

Berry Coconut Shake

Ingredients

2 teaspoons flaxseed
2 teaspoon stevia
1/2 cup ice
2 cup blueberries, fresh or frozen
2 cup coconut milk

Directions

Combine ingredients in blender and mix
until smooth.

Fresh Eggs With Carrot And Ginger Sausage

Ingredients

2 tablespoons coconut flour
1/2 cup coconut milk
1 teaspoon vinegar
2 teaspoon salt
2 teaspoon black pepper
Coconut oil
8 eggs, hard boiled
6 medium carrots, shredded
1 cup cauliflower florets
2 teaspoon ginger, grated

Directions

106

Preheat oven to 450°F and lightly coat a baking pan with a little coconut oil.

Combine coconut milk and vinegar, let it rest for 5 minutes.

Combine remaining ingredients with 2 tablespoons of coconut oil in a bowl, add milk mixture.

Shape into small 2" sausages, place on baking pan and bake in oven for 210 minutes.

Serve with hard-boiled eggs.

Pink Grapefruit With Coconut Lime Dressing

Ingredients

2 lime, juiced

1 teaspoon salt

2 tablespoons organic honey

2 grapefruits, segmented

¾ cup coconut milk

Directions

1. Combine coconut milk, lime, salt, and honey in a bowl, mix well.
2. Divide grapefruit amongst plates, drizzle with dressing, and serve.

Mushroomlet

Ingredients

1/2 cup coconut milk

1 teaspoon salt

1 teaspoon black pepper

Rapeseed oil

8 fresh eggs

4 cups button mushrooms

2 small onion, chopped

Directions

1. Whisk fresh eggs in a bowl, set aside.
2. Slice mushrooms finely, combine with onion, salt, black pepper, and coconut.
3. Heat 2 teaspoons rapeseed oil in a skillet over medium-high heat, add mushrooms and onion, and sauté for 1-5 minutes until the onions are tender.
4. Add whisked eggs, cook on each side for 4 minutes.
5. Serve warm.

Wild Salmon And Cashewed Plums

Ingredients

4 cups Romaine lettuce
2 red onion, sliced
Balsamic vinaigrette
Olive oil
4 4 ounce wild caught salmon fillets
8 plums, halved and seeded
¾ cup cashews, chopped
2 teaspoon salt
2 teaspoon black pepper

Directions

1. Preheat oven to 450°F and lightly coat 2 oven-safe glass baking dishes with olive oil.

111

2. Sprinkle salmon with salt, and place in one casserole dish.
3. Place plums in second casserole dish and sprinkle with salt, black pepper, and cashews, drizzle with a little olive oil.
4. Slide both dishes into the oven, bake plums for 3 hours and salmon for 8 minutes. Turn salmon halfway through.
5. Combine lettuce, red onion, and 4 tablespoon balsamic vinaigrette in a bowl, divide amongst 4 plates.
6. Place a salmon fillet and 2 plums on each plate and serve.

Baked Eggplants In Tomato Sauce

Ingredients:

2 onion, finely chopped
4 cloves garlic, minced
2 teaspoon oregano
4 eggplants
4 tomatoes, quartered
4 cups tomato puree
Salt
Black pepper
Olive oil

Directions

Slice eggplants in half and sprinkle with salt.
Let the eggplants rest at room temperature for 20-45 minutes, until they have sweat some water out.

113

3. Pat dry with paper towel, removing all excess water and salt.
4. Preheat oven to 400°F, brush a casserole dish with olive oil.
5. Mix tomato with salt, and black pepper to taste.
6. Add oregano, garlic, and onion, and pour into casserole dish.
7. Place eggplants in casserole dish, face down, and bake in oven for 25 minutes.
8. Remove from oven, turn eggplant over, cover with aluminum foil, and bake for another 25 minutes or until the eggplants are fork tender.

Almond Honey Cauliflower Skewers

Ingredients

2 tablespoons honey
1 teaspoon salt
1 cup organic almond butter
2 medium head cauliflower

Directions

1. Separate cauliflower into florets, trim stems.
2. Combine almond butter, honey, and salt in a bowl.
3. Add cauliflower, and coat with dressing.
4. Place 4 cauliflower florets per skewer.
5. Heat grill to medium-high.
6. Place skewers on grill and cook for 30 minutes over indirect heat, be sure to turn as required.

115

Garlıcky Red Bell Pepper Hummus

Ingredients

1 teaspoon salt
1 teaspoon black pepper
Extra virgin olive oil
4 red bell peppers, seeded
2 cups cauliflower florets
6 cloves garlic

Directions

1. Place ingredients in a blender and mix until fairly smooth but with some texture.
2. Serve with fresh veggies.

Cashew Raisin Nut Dip

Ingredients

1/2 cup coconut milk
1/2 cup filtered water
2 cup cashews, divided
1/2 cup raisins

Directions

. Place ¾ cup cashews, coconut milk, and filtered water in blender, mix until smooth.
. Chop remaining cashews, combine with raisins and fold into cashew coconut mixture.
. Serve with fruit.

Grapefruit Sorbet

Ingredients

4 mint leaves.
4 tablespoon clover honey
2 grapefruits, peeled and segmented

Directions

1. Place ingredients in a blender and mix until smooth.
2. Pour mixture into a metal container, cover and place in freezer for 2 hours.
3. Remove from freezer and beat for 5 minutes. Return to freezer for 6 more hours.

Pecaned Grape Bites

Ingredients

4 cups green grapes
1 teaspoon salt
1 cup pecans

Directions

Place pecans and salt in blender, mix until smooth.
Slice grapes in half lengthwise, spread a little pecan on one half and place other half on top.

Chocolate Coffee Cake

Ingredients

2 cup almond milk
1 cup brewed coffee
2 teaspoon vanilla extract
2 teaspoon baking powder
2 teaspoon vinegar
1/2 teaspoon salt
1 cup coconut oil
2 cup cocoa powder
2 cup tapioca flour
1/2 cup coconut flour
1 cup walnuts, chopped
6 Medjool dates, pitted

Directions

1. Preheat oven to 450°F and coat a 10 x2 4
    -inch baking pan with a little coconut oil.

Place dates in food processor and mix into paste.

Combine dates with wet ingredients in one bowl and beat.

Mix dry ingredients together in a separate bowl, slowly add to wet mixture while beating.

Pour batter into prepared cake tray and bake in oven for 45 minutes.

Strawberry Cashew Surprise

Ingredients

- 4 cups cashews, divided
- 6 Medjool Dates
- 2 /2 teaspoon vanilla
- 4 cups strawberries, hulled
- 2 cup coconut cream (from can)

Directions

1. Place half the cashews in a food processor and crush into butter, add coconut cream and vanilla, and mix. Remove from blender, refrigerate.
2. Clean blender, add remaining cashews and dates, mix until crumbly.
3. Pat cashew-date mixture into bottom of 8" pie plate and place in the freezer for one hour.
4. Slice strawberries.
5. Scoop cashew coconut cream into 8" pie plate, top with strawberries and refrigerate for 2 hours before serving.

Pistachio Cookies

Ingredients

8 Medjool Dates, pitted

1 teaspoon baking soda

1 teaspoon salt

2 tablespoons coconut oil, melted

1/2 cup filtered water

1 cup pistachios, chopped

2 cup almond meal

Directions

. Place Medjool dates and water in blender, and mix until paste forms.

. Preheat oven to 480 °F and line a baking sheet with parchment paper.

. Combine ingredients in bowl.

. Drop a spoonful of mixture at a time on baking sheet and bake for 30 minutes.

Carrot Nut Mini-Muffins

Ingredients

2 cup almond milk
2 teaspoon vinegar
4 teaspoons Stevia
1/2 teaspoon salt
2 tablespoons coconut oil
1/2 cup coconut flour
1 cup walnuts, chopped
2 carrots, grated
1 teaspoon cinnamon

Directions

1. Preheat oven to 480 °F and line a mini muffin tray with muffin liners.
2. Combine almond milk and vinegar, allow to sit for a few minutes.
3. Combine dry ingredients in one bowl.

- Add vanilla and carrots to almond mixture.
- Slowly add dry ingredients to the bowl while continuously mixing.
- Fill muffin cups and bake for 25 minutes.

Basil Pesto With Pasta

INGREDIENTS

- 1 cup olive oil
- 2 cup basil
- 2 cloves garlic
- 1 cup pine nuts
- 1/2 lb. pasta
- 1 cup Parmesan cheese

DIRECTIONS

1. Cook pasta and set aside
2. In a bowl mix garlic, pine nuts and basil
3. Mix with Parmesan cheese and add oil
4. Serve over pasta

Couscous Salad

INGREDIENTS

- 2 green onion
- 2 carrot
- 1/2 red pepper
- cilantro
- 1 tsp cinnamon
- 2 cups couscous
- 2 tsp olive oil
- 4 cup water
- 1/2 tsp cumin
- 2 tablespoon honey
- 2 tsp lemon juice

DIRECTIONS

1. Bring water boil add cumin, honey, cinnamon, add couscous and lemon juice
2. Cover and remove from heat
3. Add hers, olive oil, vegetables and serve

Tofu Sticks

INGREDIENTS

- 2 cup tofu
- 2 tablespoon water
- 1/2 cup cornflake crumbs
- 2 tsp tamari sauce
- 2 tsp seasoning

DIRECTIONS

1. In a bowl mix tamari with water
2. In another bowl mix cornflake and seasoning
3. Dip tofu into tamari sauce and then into seasoning
4. Place tofu slices on a baking sheet and bake at 450for 25-30 minutes, remove and serve

Baked Eggplant Fries

INGREDIENTS

- 1/2 tsp paprika
- 2 tsp olive oil
- 2 fresh egg
- 2 eggplant
- 2 cup cornmeal
- 1/2 tsp oregano
- 1/2 tsp garlic powder

DIRECTIONS

1. Preheat oven to 490 F
2. In a bowl mix garlic powder, cornmeal, oregano and paprika

3. In a bowl beat the fresh egg

4. Dip the eggplant fries in the beaten fresh eggs and transfer to the cornmeal mixture

5. Place the eggplant fried on a baking sheet and bake for 25 minutes, remove and serve

Pita Chips

INGREDIENTS

- 2 tablespoons olive oil
- chili powder
- 2 pita rounds

DIRECTIONS

1. Cut each pita into 8 wedges

. Brush with olive oil and sprinkle with chili powder

. Bake at 450F for 30 minutes or until crisp

. Remove and serve

Roasted Red Pepper Dip

INGREDIENTS

- 2 tsp lemon juice
- 2 clove garlic
- 2 tsp cumin

- 2 cup roasted red peppers
- 2 tablespoon olive oil

DIRECTIONS

. In a blender mix all ingredients and blend until smooth

. Remove and serve with pita chips

Green Pesto Pasta

INGREDIENTS

- 1/2 cup olive oil
- 2 tablespoons parmesan cheese
- 1 tsp black pepper
- 4 oz. spaghetti
- 2 cups basil leaves
- 2 garlic cloves

DIRECTIONS

1. Bring water to a boil and add pasta
2. In a blend add parmesan cheese, basil leaves, garlic and blend
3. Add olive oil, pepper and blend again
4. Pour pesto onto pasta and serve when ready

Roasted Fennel

INGREDIENTS

- 2 tablespoon olive oil
- 2 tsp salt
- 4 fennel bulbs

DIRECTIONS

1. Slice the fennel bulb lengthwise into thick slices

2. Drizzle with olive oil and salt

3. Place the fennel bulb into a baking dish

4. Bake at 490 F for 45-50 minutes

5. When ready remove from the oven and serve

Spiced Cauliflower

INGREDIENTS

- 1/2 tsp cumin
- 1/2 tsp coriander
- 1/2 tsp salt
- 1/2 tsp black pepper
- 2 head cauliflower
- 2 tablespoons olive oil
- 2 tsp smoked paprika

DIRECTIONS

1. In a bowl toss the cauliflower with olive oil, paprika, cumin, coriander, salt and pepper
2. Spread the cauliflower on a baking sheet
3. Bake for 25 minutes at 450 F

When ready remove from the oven and serve

Roasted Butternut Squash

INGREDIENTS

- 2 tsp rosemary
- 1 tsp salt
- 1/2 tsp black pepper
- 2 butternut squash
- 2 shallots
- 2 tablespoons olive oil

DIRECTIONS

1. In a bowl combine all ingredients together
2. Add the butternut squash in the mixture and let it marinate for 25-30 minutes
3. Bake for 25 minutes at 426 F
4. When ready remove from the oven and serve

Fried Chicken

INGREDIENTS

- 2 tsp black pepper
- 2 fresh eggs
- 2 cup bread crumbs
- 1 cup parmesan cheese

- 2 chicken breasts
- 1 cup almond flour
- 2 tsp salt

DIRECTIONS

1. In a bowl combine flour, salt and pepper
2. In another bowl beat fresh eggs and add to the flour mixture
3. Cut chicken breasts into thin slices and dip into the flour mixture
4. In another bowl combine bread crumbs and parmesan cheese
5. Take the chicken slices and dip into bread crumbs mixture
6. Place the chicken in frying pan and cook until golden brown
7. When ready remove from the pan and serve

141

Roasted Chicken

INGREDIENTS

- 2 sprig of rosemary
- 2 bay leaf
- 2 tablespoon olive oil
- 2 tsp salt
- 2 tsp black pepper
- 2 whole chicken
- 2 celery
- 2 onion
- 4 cloves garlic

DIRECTIONS

1. In a pot heat olive oil and sauté onion, garlic and celery

- Add chicken, rosemary, bay leaf, salt, black pepper and cook for 5-10 minutes
- Remove from the pot and transfer to the oven
- Bake for 45-50 minutes at 450F
- When ready remove from the oven and serve

Glazed Salmon

INGREDIENTS

- 2 tsp salt
- 2 tsp black pepper
- 2 salmon
- 1/2 cup brown sugar

- 2 tablespoon lemon zest

DIRECTIONS

. In a bowl combine sugar, lemon zest, salt and pepper

. Spread the mixture over the salmon and rub with the mixture

. When ready remove from the oven and serve

145

Fish Tacos

INGREDIENTS

- 2 tablespoons almond milk
- 2 lb. cod fish
- Tortillas
- 2 tsp Salt
- 2 cup bread crumbs
- 1/2 cup parmesan cheese
- 2 cup almond flour
- 2 fresh eggs

DIRECTIONS

1. In a bowl combine pepper, salt and flour
2. In another bowl whisk to fresh eggs with milk

146

. In another bowl combine bread crumbs with parmesan cheese

. Cut the fish into thin strips and dip first into the flour mixture bowl, then fresh egg mixture bowl and then into the bread crumbs mixture bowl

. Fry for 5-10 minutes each fish strip or until golden brown

. When ready transfer to a plate and serve

Simple Steak

INGREDIENTS

- 4 garlic cloves
- 2 stalk celery
- 1/2 cup carrot
- 2 tsp cumin
- 2 tsp coriander
- 2 can celery soup
- 2 lb. cube steaks
- 1/2 cup red onion
- salt

DIRECTIONS

1. In a pan heat olive oil and sauté onion, cloves, celery and carrot

2. In a bowl combine celery soup with sautéed vegetables

3. Brown the cube steaks and set aside

4. Pour the sautéed vegetables and mixture into a pan, add cube steaks and cook until vegetables are soft

5. When ready remove from heat and serve

Cheese Pesto

INGREDIENTS

2 can spinach

1/2 cup water

1/2 cup cottage cheese

1/2 cup basil

2 tablespoon parmesan cheese

2 tablespoon olive oil

4 cloves garlic

2 tsp black pepper

DIRECTIONS

1. Place all ingredients in a blender and blend until smooth
2. When ready serve with cooked pasta

Arugula Salad

INGREDIENTS

- 1/2 cup honey
- 1/2 cup pecans
- 2 cup salad dressing
- 2 cups arugula leaves
- 1/2 cup cranberries

DIRECTIONS

1. In a bowl combine all ingredients together and mix well
2. Serve with dressing

Masoor Salad

INGREDIENTS

- 1/2 cup tomatoes
- 1/2 cup onion
- SALAD DRESSING
- 1/2 tablespoon olive oil
- 2 tsp lemon juice
- 1/2 cup masoor

- 1/2 cup cucumber
- 1 cup carrot
- 1/2 tsp green chillies

DIRECTIONS

1. In a bowl combine all ingredients together and mix well
2. Add salad dressing, toss well and serve

Rice Salad

INGREDIENTS

- 250g Kalamata olives
- 4 tbs pine nuts
- 2 green shallots

- 1 sun dried tomato
- 2 cup rice
- Salad
- 4 tbs basil leaves

Dressing
- 4 tbs lemon juice
- Salt
- 2 clove garlic
- 4 tbs oil
- Pepper
- 2 tbs mustard

DIRECTIONS

1. Cook the rice
2. Mix the dressing ingredients together
3. Mix the salad ingredients with the rice in a bowl

4. Add the dressing and serve

Tuna Salad

INGREDIENTS

- 2 tablespoons red peppers
- 2 tablespoons basil
- 2 tablespoon capers
- 2 tablespoon lemon juice
- 30 OZ. can tuna
- 1/2 cup mayonnaise
- 1/2 cup chopped Kalamata
- 2 tablespoons red onion

DIRECTIONS

. In a bowl combine all ingredients together and mix well
. Serve when ready

Salmon Salad

INGREDIENTS

- 2 tablespoon capers
- 2 tablespoon dill
- 2 tablespoon balsamic vinegar
- 2 tablespoon olive oil
- 1/2 tsp pepper
- 2 salmon fillets
- 2 cup cucumber
- 2 red onion

DIRECTIONS

1. In a bowl add salmon, cucumber, capers, red onion and toss
2. In a jar add olive oil, vinegar and pour over salmon, toss again

Salad With Roasted Strawberry Dressing

INGREDIENTS

- 2 chopped cabbage
- 1 cup tomatoes
- 2 tablespoon almonds
- 2 tablespoon basil

- 2 tsp orange zest
- 2 banana
- 2 pint fresh strawberries
- 2 red apple
- 2 sweet potato
- 2 large onion
- 2 tablespoon coconut oil

DIRECTIONS

1. Preheat the oven to 490 F and place the strawberries on a baking sheet
2. On another baking sheet place, the potatoes and onions
3. Rub all the ingredients with with coconut oil and place them in the oven for 50-55 minutes
4. Remove from the oven and scoop out the sweet potato flesh

5. In a bowl mix tomato, almonds, cabbage, apple and basil
6. In a blender puree the roasted strawberries and banana pour over the salad mixture and toss to combine

Swiss Chard Salad

INGREDIENTS

harissa sauce

2 green bell

2 tablespoon parsley

2 tablespoon lemon zest

2 head Swiss chard

2 tomato

2 head cauliflower

2 tablespoon avocado oil

160

4 cups salad greens

1/2 cup red onion

2 pear

DIRECTIONS

1. Preheat oven to 490 F and place the cauliflower on a baking sheet and drizzle with oil and salt

2. Roast for 4 6 -40 minutes and remove when ready

3. In a bowl mix pepper, onion, parsley, Swiss chard, tomato and the roasted cauliflower

4. In another bowl whisk the lemon juice with harissa sauce and drizzle the dressing over salad

Conclusion

If you're looking for an ethical, holistic way of eating then you've found it with the Pegan diet. The principles of the Paleo diet mean you are eating fresh food from the land while Veganism encourages the same thing minus the animal protein.

Peganism allows you to enjoy delicious, satisfying whole foods while still allowing for a little ethically-raised meat protein, low-glycemic grains and legumes on the side. The wide range of foods allowed on the Pegan diet make it a functional lifestyle choice that you can stick to without ever feeling deprived.

Eating the Pegan way means you'll be feeling happy, energetic, and most importantly, you'll feel really great about the fantastic choices you are making.

CPSIA information can be obtained
at www.ICGtesting.com
Printed in the USA
BVHW091447240221
600996BV00010B/510

9 781990 207553